DEDICATI

To Yaalibapa, my hand-holder, light-illuminator, hope-giver, peace bringer, spiritual father...without whose grace I would be forever lost.

AND

To my darling babies, Aaryan, Ayra, Arham and Aarav, who turned me from someone into a mother!

My Child,

GOD LOVES YOU.

Everything is a gift from Him to you.

My Darling,

ACCEPT GOOD ADVICE.

It will help remove all your vice.

My Dear,

HAVE STRONG

FAITH.

This will lead you
to heaven's gate.

My Love,

LET TRUTH FLOW.

Never talk about things

you don't know.

My Sweetheart,

EMBRACE PATIENCE TIGHTLY.

Even the darkest moments will then shine brightly.

My Honey,

ALWAYS BE FAIR.

Side with justice

everytime, everywhere.

My Baby,

CONVERSE WITH GOD.

His is the only answer you shall ever want.

My Cutie,

NEVER STOP LEARNING.

Keep the desire
for knowledge burning.

My Boo,
SEEK HIS GUIDANCE.
Learn to read even His silence.

My Bubba,

JUST BE

KIND.

Only let good thoughts

enter your mind.

My Sweetie,

BULLYING IS BAD.

If you see it, stop it and take a stand.

My Joy,

BEAR IN MIND,

behind all your success
it is God you will find.

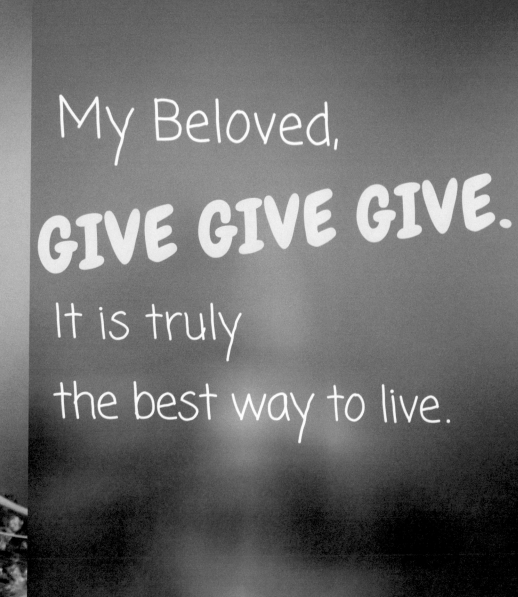

My Beloved,

GIVE GIVE GIVE.

It is truly
the best way to live.

My Angel,
IF YOU SIN,
apologize and beg
forgiveness from Him.

My Sunshine,

MAKE HONEST FRIENDS.

With them set positive trends.

My Light,

ANGER IS BAD.

Calmly find a solution,
try not to be mad.

My Precious,

TRY BEING WISE.

Stay away from vanity and pride.

My Treasured,

TREAT OTHERS

WELL.

Even in their heart,
does God dwells.

My Everything,

FAMILY COMES

FIRST.

Always love them
and never break their trust.

My Heart,

REMEMBER THESE

LINES.

Follow them daily
so your soul can shine.

Inspiration for the book

I first came across the letter of Imam Ali to his son two decades ago in a Sufi book called, "When You Hear Hoofbeats, Think of a Zebra" by Shems Friedlander (I highly recommend every parent to read it).

Since then, it has been my guide on how to conduct myself in a way that would make God happy. The letter contains everything from advice on how to treat family, friends and foes. It explains how to behave, when to talk, when to be silent, and also addresses deeper questions like what is the purpose of life.

Since I became a mother, I have been looking for ways to instill these values in my children, and do it in a way that they could internalize the messages. That formed the basis for, "My Baby, Be Good!" I hope you enjoy the book, and that both you and your loved ones learn something from it.

Saniya Bhamani

saniya.bhamani@icloud.com

Made in the USA
Columbia, SC
24 July 2024